4/14 $26

Lucius Beebe Memorial Library
345 Main Street
Wakefield, MA 01880
(781) 246-6334
www.wakefieldlibrary.org

Explore the Solar System

Galaxies and the Universe

WORLD
BOOK

a Scott Fetzer company
Chicago
www.worldbookonline.com

World Book, Inc.
233 N. Michigan Avenue
Chicago, IL 60601
U.S.A.

For information about other World Book publications, visit
our website at **http://www.worldbookonline.com** or call
1-800-WORLDBK (967-5325).

For information about sales to schools and
libraries, call **1-800-975-3250 (United States)**,
or **1-800-837-5365 (Canada)**.

Library of Congress Cataloging-in-Publication data
Galaxies and the universe.
   p. cm. -- (Explore the solar system)
   Summary: "An introduction to galaxies and the universe for
primary and intermediate grade students, with information
about their formation and features. Includes a list of highlights
for each chapter, fun facts, glossary, resource list, and index" --
Provided by publisher.
   Includes index.
   ISBN 978-0-7166-9542-4
   1. Galaxies--Juvenile literature. 2. Solar system--Juvenile
literature. 3. Astronomy--Juvenile literature. I. World Book, Inc.
   QB857.3.G352 2011
   523.1'12--dc22

                              2010014486

ISBN 978-0-7166-9533-2 (set)
Printed in China by Leo Paper Products Ltd.,
   Heshan, Guangdong
2nd printing February 2012

Staff
Executive Committee
President:
   Donald D. Keller
Vice President and Editor in Chief: Paul A. Kobasa
Vice President, Marketing/Digital Products:
   Sean Klunder
Vice President, Licensing & Business Development:
   Richard Flower
Controller: Yan Chen
Director, Human Resources: Bev Ecker

Editorial:
Associate Director, Supplementary Publications:
   Scott Thomas
Managing Editor, Supplementary Publications:
   Barbara A. Mayes
Senior Editor, Supplementary Publications:
   Kristina A. Vaicikonis
Researcher, Supplementary Publications:
   Annie Brodsky
Manager, Contracts & Compliance
   (Rights & Permissions): Loranne K. Shields
Editor: Michael DuRoss
Writer: Dan Blunk
Indexer: David Pofelski

Manufacturing/Production/Graphics and Design:
Director: Carma Fazio
Manufacturing Manager: Steven K. Hueppchen
Production/Technology Manager: Anne Fritzinger
Proofreader: Emilie Schrage
Manager, Graphics and Design: Tom Evans
Coordinator, Design Development
   and Production: Brenda B. Tropinski
Associate Designer: Matt Carrington
Contributing Photographs Editor: Carol Parden

Picture Acknowledgments:
Cover front: NASA/Hubble Heritage Team (STScI/AURA)/ESA/S. Beckwith
(STScI)/Robert Gendler (Additional Processing); Cover back: NASA/JPL-Caltech/UCLA.

© David Jepson/Alamy Images 45; © Richard Wainscoat, Alamy Images 22; © David Malin,
Anglo-Australian Observatory 19; © John Gleason, Celestial 8; ESA 51: ESO 4, 38;
howstuffworks.com 25; JPL 55; Millennium Simulation Project 30; NASA 12, 29, 41;
NASA/Chandra X-Ray Telescope 46, 50; NASA/CXC/cFAVE 36, 52; NASA/CXC/MIT 20;
NASA/ESA 19, 43; NASA/ESA/Hubble Heritage Team 26, 27, 47, 49, 54; NASA/StScI/AURA
1, 6, 29; NASA/WMAPScience Team 33; © Mark Garlick, SPL/Photo Researchers 10; © David A.
Hardy, Futures: 50 Years in Space/SPL/Photo Researchers 15; The Science Museum, Oxford 45;
WYN/NOAO/AIRA/NSF 42.

Illustrations: WORLD BOOK illustrations by Matt Carrington 16, 35, 39, 53; WORLD BOOK
illustration by Paul Perreault 59.

Astronomers use different kinds of photos to learn about such objects in space as planets.
Many photos show an object's natural color. Other photos use false colors. Some false-color
images show types of light the human eye cannot normally see. Others have colors that were
changed to highlight important features. When appropriate, the captions in this book state
whether a photo uses natural or false color.

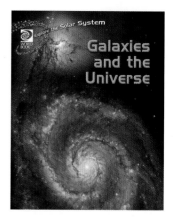

Cover image:
The swirling arms of the
Whirlpool Galaxy, one of the
best-known spiral galaxies,
contain millions of stars.

Contents

If a word is printed in **bold letters that look like this,** that word's meaning is given in the glossary on pages 60-61.

What Is a Galaxy?

A **galaxy** is a collection of gas, dust, **stars,** and other **matter** held together by **gravity.** A good way to think of a galaxy is as an island of matter in the vast emptiness of space.

Galaxies are huge. The largest may be 6 million **light-years** across. A light-year is the distance light travels in one year—about 5.88 trillion miles (9.46 trillion kilometers).

After years of discovering and studying galaxies, **astronomers** have learned that galaxies come in many shapes and sizes. No two are exactly alike.

Fun Fact

Some scientists estimate that there may be 60 galaxies in the universe for every person alive on Earth today.

Highlights

- A galaxy is a collection of gas, dust, and stars.
- The largest galaxies may be more than 6 million light-years across.
- Galaxies come in many different shapes and sizes.
- No two galaxies are exactly alike.

Stars shine in a false-color image of a spiral galaxy made up of several photographs taken with the Hubble Space Telescope.

What Are Galaxies Made Of?

Galaxies contain huge numbers of **stars. Astronomers** and other scientists first discovered and learned about galaxies by observing the light from stars.

But galaxies are made of much more than stars. They also contain such things as **planets, moons, asteroids,** and huge clouds of gas and dust. All of these objects have one thing in common—they are made of a type of **matter** that is *visible* (that can be seen). Matter is visible if it either gives off, reflects, or *absorbs* (takes in) light.

Galaxies also contain another type of matter that is much different from visible matter. This type of matter is called **dark matter.** It does not give off, reflect, or absorb light, and so

Highlights

- Galaxies contain both visible and invisible matter.
- Matter is visible when it either gives off or reflects light.
- Matter that does not give off, reflect, or absorb light is called dark matter.
- Scientists think dark matter makes up most of the mass of the universe.

it cannot be seen directly with a telescope. Scientists think that dark matter makes up most of the **mass** (amount of matter) in the **universe.** Although they cannot see dark matter, scientists know it is there because they have seen the effects of its **gravity** on other objects.

The Sombrero Galaxy in a natural-color image made up of several photographs taken by the Hubble Space Telescope

Which Galaxy Are We In?

Highlights

- The solar system is located in a galaxy called the Milky Way.
- Ancient people gave the Milky Way this name because when they looked at the sky, they saw a white haze that looked like spilled milk.
- The white haze is the light from stars that are too far away to be seen individually.

A portion of the Milky Way Galaxy in a natural-color photograph

The **solar system,** which includes the sun, Earth, and the other **planets** in **orbit** around the sun, is located in a **galaxy** called the Milky Way. The Milky Way Galaxy contains hundreds of billions of other **stars** besides the sun, as well as huge clouds of dust and gas.

On a dark night, we can see distant parts of the Milky Way from Earth. The individual stars in some regions are too far away to be seen without a telescope. But the light from the stars appears as a white haze that looks like a river of spilled milk. Ancient people gave our galaxy its name before anyone knew what it was. The stars we can see make up a very small number of all the stars in the galaxy!

What Is the Shape of the Milky Way?

The Milky Way **Galaxy** is shaped like a thin disk with a bulge in the center. The bulge consists of a vast, thick bar of **stars** as well as gas, dust, and other **matter.** Several "arms" swirl outward from the bulge. Because of these arms, the Milky Way is known as a **spiral** galaxy. If you were looking down on the Milky Way from above, it would look somewhat like a pinwheel.

The galaxy's arms also contain stars and gas and dust. Most of the youngest stars in the galaxy can be found there. Most of the oldest stars are in two flattened spheres of stars that surround the bulge and disk. These spheres are called halos.

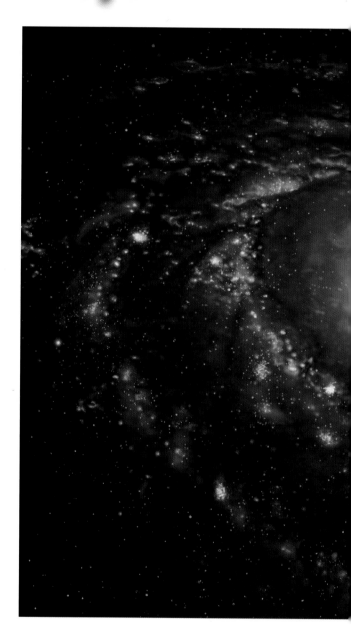

The Milky Way is shaped like a disk, with a bulge in the center and arms that spiral outward from the center.

How Big Is the Milky Way?

The Milky Way is enormous. If you could travel at the **speed of light,** it would take you 100,000 years to get from one end of the **galaxy** to the other! Light travels about 5.88 trillion miles (9.46 trillion kilometers)—in one year.

The central bulge of the Milky Way is about 10,000 **light-years** thick and about 27,000 light-years long. Toward the edges, the Milky Way is about 1,000 light-years thick. Scientists think that the galaxy contains about 200 billion **stars.** The Milky Way is so massive that there are many smaller **galaxies** in **orbit** around it, much like **moons** orbiting a **planet.**

Fun Fact

The Milky Way's central bulge is made up of a thick bar of stars that stretches for about 27,000 light-years. That is why astronomers call the Milky Way a barred spiral galaxy.

Although the Milky Way is vast, other galaxies are even larger. The most massive galaxies can have 100 times as much **mass** —in the form of stars, hot gas, and other **matter**—as the Milky Way.

Highlights

- The Milky Way is so large, it would take someone traveling at the speed of light 100,000 years to travel from one end of the galaxy to the other.

- The Milky Way contains about 200 billion stars.

- Some galaxies are even larger than the Milky Way.

The central bulge of the Milky Way appears in a photo taken from the side by a satellite recording *infrared light* (light in the form of heat).

Where Is the Solar System In the Milky Way?

Long ago, people thought that our **planet** was at the center of the **universe.** They thought that all the other planets and even the sun **orbited** around Earth. Today, we know that Earth is not the center of the **solar system** or the **Milky Way Galaxy.**

The solar system is actually located in one of the outer arms of the Milky Way. This arm is called the Orion arm. Earth is very far—about 25,000 **light-years**—from the center of the galaxy. In Earth's part of the galaxy, **stars** are, on average, about five light-years away from one another. Nearer to the center of the galaxy, stars are about 100 times as close to each other. For this reason, the center of the galaxy appears extremely bright.

Highlights

- People once thought that Earth was at the center of the solar system and the galaxy.
- Today we know that the solar system is on one of the outer arms of the Milky Way.
- Earth is about 25,000 light-years from the center of the Milky Way.

The solar system

The Milky Way Galaxy viewed from above in an artist's illustration

The solar system

The Milky Way Galaxy viewed from the side

How Did the Solar System Form in the Milky Way?

The solar system began as a giant cloud of dust and gas (1). The cloud collapsed inward because of the pull of gravity and became a flattened disk (2). Some of the dust particles in the disk collided and began to form larger bodies (3). Some of these small bodies grew to become planets (4).

Astronomers believe that about 5 billion years ago the **solar system** was just a giant, rotating cloud of dust and gas. Then this cloud began to collapse under the pull of its own **gravity.** Many astronomers think that a nearby exploding star called a **supernova** triggered this collapse. As the cloud fell in on itself, gas and dust began to spin faster and flatten out. Eventually, the cloud became a large disk of **matter.**

The disk continued to collapse under its own weight and to draw in more gas and dust. At the center of the disk, the gravity was so strong that *particles* (pieces) of dust were pulled together closely. The pressure became great enough to trigger **nuclear fusion reactions.** This process caused the sun to begin shining as a **star.**

In a similar way, fragments of rock in the disk combined to create the rocky inner **planets**— Mercury, Venus, Earth, and Mars. Gases, dust, and ice farther from the sun collected to form the huge **gas giants**—Jupiter, Saturn, Uranus, and Neptune. According to this theory, **asteroids** and **comets** are made of material that was left over after the formation of the sun and planets.

Highlights

- **The solar system began to form about 5 billion years ago.**
- **A cloud of gas and dust in the Milky Way collapsed under its own gravity and formed a disk.**
- **Eventually, the inner planets formed from colliding bits of rock. The outer gas giants formed when gases and dust froze far from the sun.**

What Other Galaxies Are Near the Milky Way?

The Milky Way is part of the Local Group, a collection of about 30 nearby **galaxies.** Two of these nearby galaxies—Andromeda (an DROM uh duh) and M33—are large **spiral** galaxies like the Milky Way. The Local Group also contains two other galaxies called the Large Magellanic (MAJ uh LAN ihk) Cloud and the Small Magellanic Cloud. These galaxies are visible from Earth as small, hazy patches.

About 55 million **light-years** from the Local Group is an even larger grouping of **stars** called the Virgo Cluster. This cluster is named after the **constellation** Virgo. The Virgo Cluster and the constellation Virgo appear in the same part of Earth's night sky. However, the stars that make up the Virgo constellation are in the Milky Way.

The Local Group and the Virgo Cluster are part of an even larger group of galaxies called the Local Supercluster. The supercluster contains tens of thousands of galaxies. Scientists have discovered that superclusters are arranged in chains. They are separated by huge spaces where no galaxies exist.

Highlights

- The Milky Way is part of a group of galaxies called the Local Group.
- The Local Group is part of a larger collection of galaxies called the Virgo Cluster.
- And the Virgo Cluster is in an even larger group called the Local Supercluster.

Galaxy M33 (inset), located
about 2.5 million light-years
from the Milky Way, is also a
spiral galaxy and one of the
Milky Way's closest neighbors.

The Small Magellanic Cloud, like
the Milky Way, belongs to the
Local Group of galaxies.

How Does the Milky Way Travel Through Space?

At the center of the Milky Way lies a small object with a huge mass called Sagittarius A*. Scientists think the object may be a black hole. The bright areas in this image represent X rays given off by Sagittarius A*.

20 Explore the Solar System

The Milky Way, like the **solar system**, is constantly moving. Like **planets orbiting** the sun, **stars** and other objects in the Milky Way orbit the center of the **galaxy.**

The Milky Way is so huge that it takes the sun about 250 million years to complete one orbit around the galactic center! Other stars may take more or less time to complete an orbit, depending on how far they are from the center.

Astronomers have studied the orbit of the stars in the Milky Way using powerful **instruments.** These devices include telescopes that detect radio waves—a type of **electromagnetic energy.** Scientists have discovered that everything in the Milky Way is orbiting a small object with a huge amount of **mass** in the exact center of the galaxy. Scientists believe this object, called Sagittarius (*SAJ uh TAIR ee uhs*) A*, may be a black hole. A black hole is a region of space so dense that nothing can escape its **gravity,** not even light.

Highlights

- The Milky Way is constantly in motion.
- All of the stars and other objects in the Milky Way orbit the galaxy's center.
- At the center of the Milky Way is a small object with a huge mass called Sagittarius A*.
- Scientists think Sagittarius A* is a black hole.

What Is Special About the Milky Way?

In some ways, the Milky Way seems to be pretty ordinary. It is only one of hundreds of billions of **galaxies** in the **universe.** In addition, the Milky Way does not look much different from the many other **spiral** galaxies. And as galaxies go, the Milky Way is not even particularly large.

But the Milky Way has one very remarkable thing going for it. The **solar system,** which includes the sun and the **planet** Earth, is part of the Milky Way. Earth is the only place we know of that has life. The Milky Way is special to us because it is our home.

Highlights

- The Milky Way is a spiral galaxy that is not much different from other spiral galaxies.
- But the Milky Way is special because it contains Earth, the only place in the universe we know of that contains life.

The Milky Way arcs across the sky above the Keck I telescope dome at the Mauna Kea Observatory in Hawaii.

How Do Galaxies Form?

Most scientists believe that early in the history of the **universe, matter** was spread out fairly evenly. However, there were pockets of a mysterious substance called **dark matter.** These lumpy regions acted as the "seeds" for the formation of **galaxies.**

The dark matter's **gravity** pulled in vast clouds of the gas that filled the universe. These clouds began to spin and grow larger, forming bodies known as protogalaxies. The protogalaxies pulled in more and more of the surrounding gas and dust. Eventually, the protogalaxies became dense enough to collapse inward and form **stars.**

When two protogalaxies combined or collided, the force triggered new bursts of star formation. Repeated collisions between small galaxies eventually formed large galaxies such as the Milky Way. Galaxies are still combining and colliding today.

Highlights

- Lumps of dark matter became the seeds around which galaxies began to form.
- The clouds surrounding the dark matter formed bodies called protogalaxies.
- Eventually, protogalaxies became dense enough to collapse and begin forming stars.
- Large galaxies formed from collisions between small galaxies.

Evolution of a Galaxy

According to one model, spiral galaxies form in much the same way as stars form.

1. Gas, dust, and young stars collide.

2. The stars begin to rotate around the center of the mass.

3. The rotation causes the cloud to contract and form a disk.

4. As the disk spins, spiral arms form.

What Types of Galaxies Are There?

There are three basic kinds of **galaxies: spiral** galaxies, **elliptical** galaxies, and irregular galaxies.

Spiral galaxies look like pinwheels. They have arms filled with **stars** that twist around a central point. The Milky Way is a spiral galaxy.

Elliptical galaxies look like clouds of stars. They vary in shape from near-perfect circles to flattened globes. Elliptical galaxies are brighter at the center than they are at the edges.

Irregular galaxies are some of the strangest-looking galaxies. They can be circular in shape, but

M82, also called the Cigar Galaxy, is an irregular galaxy.

they appear to have no particular pattern of stars. Two irregular galaxies are close enough to the Milky Way to be visible without a telescope. They are called the Large Magellanic Cloud and the Small Magellanic Cloud.

Galaxy NGC 1132 (top right) is an elliptical galaxy. It is so huge that astronomers call it a giant elliptical. Galaxy NGC 1427A (above) is an irregular galaxy. It is slowly coming apart as it collides with other galaxies.

Highlights

- There are three basic types of galaxies: spiral, elliptical, and irregular.
- Spiral galaxies have arms filled with stars twisted around a central point.
- Elliptical galaxies are cloud-shaped.
- Irregular galaxies have no particular pattern of stars.

Can Galaxies Run into Each Other?

Galaxies often combine. Fast-moving galaxies can zip right through each other without much effect. If the galaxies are moving more slowly, the two may merge and form one larger galaxy.

Large galaxies often "eat up" smaller galaxies. As galaxies grow closer, the **gravity** from the larger galaxy pulls **stars** and other **matter** from the smaller galaxy toward it in long streams. The stars in colliding galaxies rarely crash into one another. Galaxies are so huge that their stars usually just fly past one another.

Astronomers have found that the Milky Way is stripping stars from two nearby galaxies. Our galaxy is also on a collision course with the Andromeda Galaxy. In several billion years, the two **spiral** galaxies will likely combine to form one **elliptical** galaxy.

Highlights

- Although galaxies are far apart in space, they often collide or combine.
- Colliding galaxies may form one large galaxy.
- The stars within colliding galaxies are so distant that they usually do not crash into one another.
- The Milky Way is stripping stars from two nearby galaxies.

Astronomers believe that Galaxy M64, also called the Black Eye Galaxy, formed when two galaxies collided.

The Milky Way (in blue, right) is slowly absorbing the Canis Major Galaxy (red), as depicted in an artist's drawing based on scientific evidence discovered in 2003.

What Is the Universe?

Galaxies appear as bright dots on strings of matter several billion light-years long in a computer *simulation* (representation) of the structure of one part of the universe. Some of the dots represent clusters of galaxies (inset).

The **universe** is everything. It is all the **stars, planets,** and **galaxies** as well as other forms of **matter.** The universe also includes *visible* light (light we can see) and other forms of **energy.**

The universe is so huge that its size is almost too big to imagine. **Astronomers** think the universe contains hundreds of billions of galaxies. But that is just the number of galaxies they -think exist in the observable universe, or the part of the universe that can be seen from Earth (see page 34). Even if you could move at the **speed of light,** it would take billions of years to travel to the most distant galaxies we can see.

Since the early 1800's, we have begun to learn how the universe is organized. It is arranged into galaxies and groupings of galaxies called superclusters. Networks of galaxies called filaments stream across vast distances of space.

Despite the presence of all the stars and galaxies, most of the universe is nearly empty of any visible matter.

Highlights

- The universe is made up of all the matter, light, and other forms of energy that exist.
- It is organized into galaxies, superclusters, and huge string-like networks of galaxies in space.
- Most of the universe is empty of visible matter.

How Old Is the Universe?

Many kinds of scientific evidence strongly suggest that the **universe** is about 13.7 billion years old. Two clues to this age are the ages of the **stars** and the movement of **galaxies.**

Astronomers know that the universe must be older than the oldest stars. They believe that stars did not begin to form until about 400,000 years after the **big bang,** the cosmic event that scientists think started the expansion of the universe. The oldest stars found so far appear to be a little over 13 billion years old. This suggests the big bang occurred about 13.7 billion years ago.

More evidence about the age of the universe comes from the movement of the galaxies. All far-away galaxies appear to be moving away from one another. Scientists know how fast the galaxies are separating. They use this information to figure out about how long it has been since these galaxies were much closer together. These calculations suggest that the universe is 13.7 billion years old.

Highlights

- Astronomers think the universe is about 13.7 billion years old.
- They figured out the age by determining the age of the oldest stars and the distance between galaxies.
- Scientists believe galaxies were once tightly packed together and that an explosion called the big bang caused them to start moving apart.

Big Bang Expansion

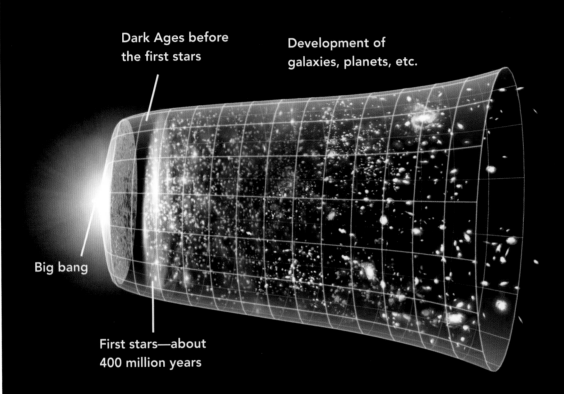

Dark Ages before
the first stars

Development of
galaxies, planets, etc.

Big bang

First stars—about
400 million years

13.7 billion years

How Big Is the Universe?

The **universe** is incredibly large. In fact, it may be impossible for **astronomers** to determine the actual size of the universe. No one knows for sure whether the universe is *finite* (limited) or infinite. *Observations* (information gained by watching) made with advanced telescopes indicate that there are hundreds of billions or even trillions of **galaxies** in the observable universe. (The observable universe is that part of the universe that we can see from Earth.)

Measurements show that the most distant galaxies observed to date are over 13 billion **light-years** from Earth. That means that light from these galaxies has been traveling through space for at least that long. So we are seeing those galaxies as they existed 13 billion years ago. There are probably galaxies even farther away whose light has not yet reached us.

Highlights

- The universe is extremely big.
- It contains at least 100 billion galaxies that we can see and more that we cannot see.
- Light takes time to travel. So when we see the light of faraway objects in space, we are really seeing those objects as they were long ago.

Light Speed

Nothing in the universe is faster than light. Light travels at the speed of 186,282 miles (299,792 kilometers) per second. At this speed, light can travel about 5.88 trillion miles (9.46 trillion kilometers) per year.

Light from the Coma Supercluster (above), a group of galaxies, can reach Earth in 300 million years.

Light from the Andromeda Galaxy (left), the nearest galaxy similar to the Milky Way, takes 2.3 million years to reach us.

Jupiter (below) is 366 million miles (589 million kilometers) from Earth. It takes light from Jupiter only 33 minutes to reach Earth.

Is the Universe Changing?

Five galaxies in a group called Stephan's Quintet are colliding and changing, as shown in an image made by combining photographs from several kinds of telescopes.

For a very long time, **astronomers** thought the **universe** never changed. One of the most important scientific discoveries of the 1900's occurred when scientists learned that the universe is actually expanding, or moving outward. Space is getting bigger all the time.

Until 1924, scientists thought that the Milky Way, our home **galaxy,** was the only galaxy in the universe. Then, American astronomer Edwin Hubble (1889-1953) studied a faint patch of light in the sky. Hubble was able to show that the light was actually a large group of **stars** that was 2 million **light-years** away—much farther away than the stars in our galaxy. Hubble's work proved that there are other galaxies beyond the Milky Way.

Highlights

- In 1924, American astronomer Edwin Hubble was the first to prove that there are other galaxies besides the Milky Way in the universe.
- Hubble also showed that the universe is expanding, one of the most important discoveries of the 1900's.

Gravity causes galaxies within the same cluster to stay close together and even at times to collide. When Hubble examined the light from distant galaxies, however, he found that those galaxies that were far from each other were growing even farther apart. In fact, the farther two galaxies are from each other, the faster the distance between them grows. To astronomers, this finding meant that the entire universe is expanding.

How Do Galaxies Move as Space Expands?

All of the **galaxies** that **astronomers** can see, except the ones closest to Earth, are moving away from us and from each other. These galaxies, however, are not moving *through* space. The space within the **universe** is expanding, or stretching. As space expands, the universe carries the galaxies along with it. The galaxies are moving *with* space. Because the universe itself is expanding, there is nothing outside the universe for the universe to expand into.

To understand this, you could compare the universe to a balloon with spots. The universe is the balloon, and the spots are galaxies. As the balloon fills with air, the surface expands and the dots move farther apart. The dots are not moving *through* the balloon; they are moving along with the surface of the balloon.

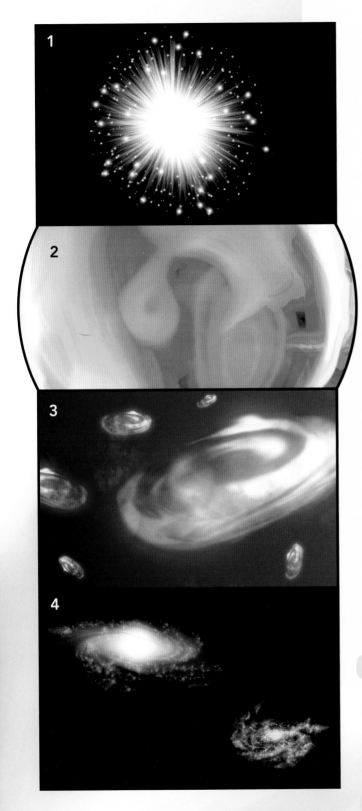

How Galaxies Move

1. Scientists believe the universe began with a huge explosion of matter and energy called the big bang.

2. Space itself came into being and expanded like an inflating balloon, carrying matter with it. Matter was crowded more closely together in some regions of space than in others.

3. The more crowded regions began to attract greater amounts of matter. Large clumps of matter began to form galaxies and clusters of galaxies. The developing galaxies continued to be carried farther away from one another as the universe expanded.

4. Today, the galaxies and galaxy clusters continue to rush away from one another as space expands.

Highlights

- Most galaxies continue to move away from each other.
- They are moving because all of space is expanding like a balloon and carrying the galaxies with it.

What Was the Big Bang?

Most **astronomers** think that the **universe** began expanding in a sudden, violent event called the **big bang.** According to this theory, the big bang marks the "birth" of the universe. Astronomers think the big bang occurred about 13.7 billion years ago (see page 32).

Like an exploding firecracker, the universe was very hot right after the big bang. As space expanded, the universe began to cool off. Eventually the universe grew cool enough for **matter** to form into **stars** and **galaxies.**

There are differences between the big bang and a firecracker explosion, however. When a firecracker explodes, the matter and force push away from the center of the firecracker. The big bang, however, happened throughout the entire universe. It pushed everything away from everything else. The big bang had no center.

A lot of evidence supports the big bang theory. Using complex **instruments, astronomers** have

Highlights

- Most scientists believe the universe began with an explosion called the big bang.
- After the big bang, the universe began to expand and cool, and matter formed into stars and galaxies.
- Bits of energy called cosmic microwave background radiation that astronomers have found in space are proof of the big bang.

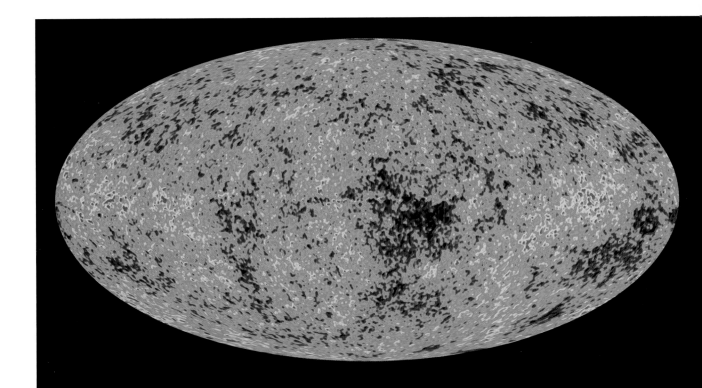

A map of the universe created by a space probe shows slight differences in temperature of the cosmic microwave background (CMB) radiation. Blue represents the coolest temperatures. Red shows the warmest. CMB radiation is the most ancient form of energy ever found. Most scientists believe that the CMB radiation is proof that the universe began with the big bang.

found small amounts of **energy** in space. Astronomers believe this energy, which is called cosmic microwave background radiation, was left over from the big bang. This energy provides the best proof we have that the universe began with a big bang.

Is the Universe Expanding Faster Than It Used To?

The **universe** has been expanding since the **big bang.** **Astronomers** once thought that **gravity** was slowing the expansion. In 1998, however, **astronomers** announced that **supernovae** in distant **galaxies** appeared dimmer than they had expected. The brightness of these exploding stars as viewed from Earth depends on their distance. That is, closer supernovae appear brighter. Scientists concluded that the dimmer supernovae were farther away than they would be if the expansion of the universe was slowing down. This suggests that the expansion is actually speeding up.

Scientists think this speeding up involves a mysterious type of **energy** called **dark energy.** Very little is known about dark energy, because it cannot be seen with telescopes or other **instruments.** Dark energy appears to work against the pull of gravity, causing the universe to expand faster and faster.

Highlights

- Scientists once believed that gravity was slowing down the expansion of the universe.
- In 1998, measurements of the brightness of distant supernovae convinced scientists that the expansion of the universe is actually speeding up.
- Scientists believe that a type of energy called dark energy is causing the universe to expand faster.

Pickering's Triangle (interior of cloud) has been formed by the remains of a supernova called the Cygnus Loop. By measuring the brightness of distant supernovae, scientists learned that the expansion of the universe is speeding up, not slowing down as they once thought.

How Have We Learned So Much About the Universe?

We have learned a lot about the **universe** by asking questions! Since ancient times, humans have tried to make sense of the world. The ancient Greeks were among the first people to use science and mathematics to explain how the natural world works. They mapped the **stars** and measured the size of Earth with surprising accuracy.

Highlights

- Ancient Greeks were among the first people to explain the natural world through science and mathematics.
- Instruments such as telescopes have helped people to study the universe.
- Many important discoveries were made with the Hubble Space Telescope.

As time went on, people learned how to make **instruments** to help them learn about the sun, Earth's **moon,** and the **planets.** For example, most of the great discoveries about how the universe is organized occurred because of the invention of complex telescopes.

Today, **astronomers** send large telescopes into space. One of the most important **orbiting** telescopes is NASA's Hubble Space Telescope. This telescope has looked farther into the universe and produced clearer images of distant objects than any other telescope before it. The Hubble is named for American astronomer Edwin Hubble, who made important contributions to astronomy in the 1920's (see page 37).

A model of the universe based on the theories of Polish astronomer Nicolaus Copernicus (1473-1543) (right) is one of many such devices used by early astronomers to study the heavens.

The domes of two of the largest telescopes in the world, Keck I and Keck II, stand on Mauna Kea, a mountain on the island of Hawaii.

How Do Astronomers Study the Universe?

Part of the center of the Milky Way in an X-ray image taken by the orbiting Chandra X-ray Observatory

Astronomers must use different **instruments** to learn about the different types of **matter** and **energy** in the **universe.** For example, dense clouds of dust and gas block our ability to see the center of the Milky Way **Galaxy** using *optical telescopes* (telescopes that gather only visible light). But many objects, including the Milky Way, give off other types of **electromagnetic energy** besides visible light. Scientists have made telescopes that can "see" all forms of energy in the **spectrum** (band of light waves). By using an X-ray telescope, for example, scientists can see through the dust and gas to learn what the center of the galaxy looks like.

Many photographs of **stars** and other astronomical objects begin as black-and-white images. Scientists add color to these photos to help them see details or to mark differences in temperatures or other characteristics. Some images collected by telescopes are simply signals that record information about light that is invisible to human eyes. In these cases, scientists add color to turn these signals into images they can understand and study.

Highlights

- Scientists have invented different kinds of telescopes to "see" objects in the universe that give off various kinds of electromagnetic energy.

- In addition to optical telescopes, which capture images in visible light, there are telescopes that "see" X rays, radio waves, and infrared light.

A false-color image of part of the Milky Way made with the Hubble Space Telescope in visible light

Galaxies and the Universe 47

What Is Dark Matter?

Dark matter is a substance that scientists think makes up most of the matter in the **universe.** Dark matter is not the same as a black hole (see page 50).

It is hard to detect dark matter. Dark matter does not shine like stars or give off any type of **electromagnetic energy**.

Dark matter cannot be seen directly with telescopes or other **instruments.** But scientists can observe the effects of its **gravity.** For instance, **galaxies** have much more gravity than can be explained by the **stars** and other **matter** that we can see. Scientists know that gravity depends on the **mass** (amount of matter) in an object. Therefore, these galaxies must have some form of invisible matter that increases their mass.

In 2007, **astronomers** made the first three-dimensional map showing dark matter in a small part of the sky. They used the Hubble Space Telescope and other telescopes to chart the positions of ordinary matter. Then they looked for areas where light was being distorted, or bent. When viewed from Earth, dark matter bends light from objects that lie behind it. The astronomers measured the distance to the dark matter based on the distortions. They used this information to create the map.

Highlights

- Scientists think that dark matter makes up most of the matter in the universe.
- Although dark matter cannot be seen with telescopes or other instruments, scientists can tell it's there by observing the effects of its gravity on other objects in space.

Dark energy, 75%

Dark matter, 21%

Normal matter, 4%

A fuzzy ring indicates the presence of dark matter in an image taken by the Hubble Space Telescope. The ring appears because light from galaxies at the center of the image is being bent by dark matter in front of them.

A pie chart showing the amount of matter and energy that some scientists believe exists in the universe

Galaxies and the Universe **49**

What Are Black Holes?

A jet of high-energy particles streams from a black hole in a nearby galaxy in an image captured by the Chandra X-ray Observatory.

Black holes are places in space where **gravity** is so strong that even light, which moves very fast, cannot escape. Black holes are not the same as **dark matter** (see page 48).

Astronomers have learned that black holes form when **stars** much larger than the sun run out of fuel. When this happens, the star collapses under its own gravity. All of its **mass** becomes concentrated in a tiny space, creating a black hole.

Scientists cannot see black holes with telescopes. However, they think black holes exist because they can see **matter** and

energy that is being drawn into them by the strong gravity of the black hole. Most astronomers think there are millions of small black holes in the Milky Way. They have also found evidence of a very powerful black hole at the center of the Milky Way and other **galaxies.**

The strong gravity of a black hole pulls a star apart, in a series of images by an artist.

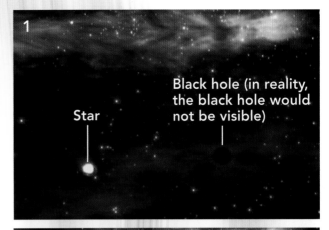

Star

Black hole (in reality, the black hole would not be visible)

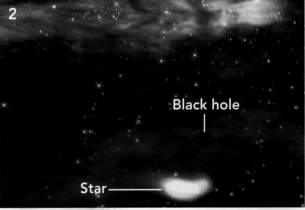

Black hole

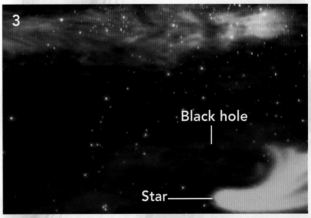

Black hole

Star

Black hole

Star

Highlights

- Black holes are places in space where stars have burned out, concentrating all of their mass into a tiny space.
- The force of gravity is so strong in such places that not even light can escape.
- Astronomers have found evidence of small black holes in the Milky Way and also of a huge black hole at the center of the Milky Way.

What Are Pulsars?

Pulsars are spinning objects in space that give off strong beams of **electromagnetic energy**. Pulsars got their name because the **energy** they give off appears to come in bursts, or pulses. The narrow beams move as the object spins, like the light from a lighthouse. We see a "pulse" each time the beam sweeps over Earth.

Pulsars spin very fast. The average pulsar spins twice every second. Over time, pulsars lose energy and slow down.

Scientists think pulsars are a type of **neutron star,** the smallest and densest type of star ever discovered. Neutron stars form when large stars run out of fuel. These stars are not massive enough to form black holes. Neutron stars are so dense that one tablespoon of material would weigh as much as 3,000 aircraft carriers.

Energy shooting from a pulsar forms a hand-like shape 150 light-years long in an image taken by the Chandra X-ray Observatory. This pulsar is only about 12 miles (19 kilometers) in diameter.

Beams of radio waves stream from both ends of a spinning pulsar in an artist's drawing. The pulsar is surrounded by an extremely powerful magnetic field that spins along with it.

Highlights

- Pulsars are the objects left over when a star runs out of fuel but is not large enough to form a black hole.

- Pulsars spin as they give off energy. The waves reach Earth as bursts, or pulses.

What Are Star Clusters?

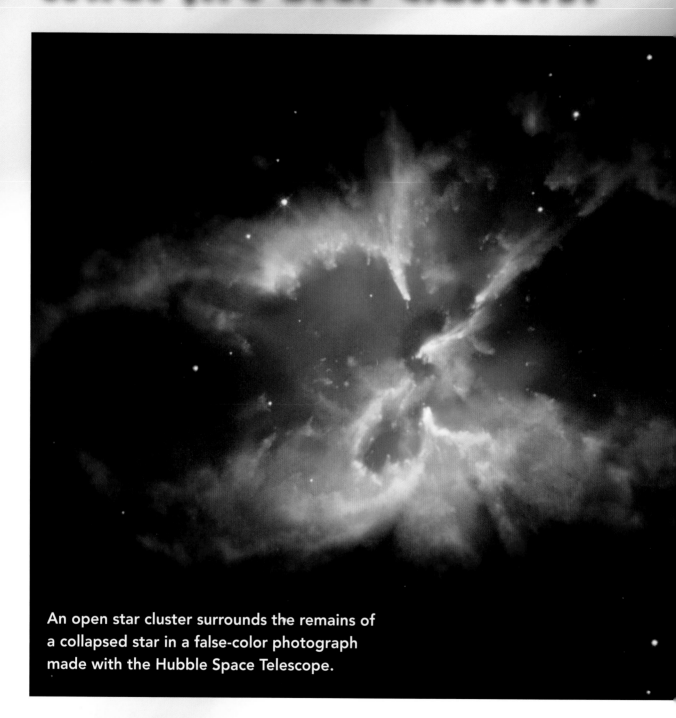

An open star cluster surrounds the remains of
a collapsed star in a false-color photograph
made with the Hubble Space Telescope.

Star clusters are large groups of stars that are found within or surrounding a **galaxy.** The clusters exist because the stars are held together by the **gravity** that attracts them to each other.

There are two types of star clusters: open clusters and globular clusters. Open clusters are loose groups of stars that are usually found near large clouds of gas and dust. The stars in open clusters are relatively young stars.

Globular clusters are groups of stars that are much closer together than the stars in open clusters. Globular clusters are usually larger than open clusters. Scientists think the stars in globular clusters are very old. Some might be as old as 12 billion years. This would make them some of the oldest known stars.

Could Life Exist Elsewhere in the Universe?

The **universe** is so huge its size is almost beyond our imagination. There are certainly plenty of places life could begin. There are hundreds of billions of **galaxies** in the observable universe. Some of these galaxies contain trillions (a million million) of **stars.** Also, scientists continue to discover **planets** circling distant stars.

In the Milky Way alone, there are probably billions of stars that are the right size and temperature to allow life to evolve on planets in **orbit** around them. Scientists do not know for sure, but they think it is possible that life could arise somewhere else in the universe. But for now, we have only found life in one place—Earth.

Highlights

- There are so many galaxies, stars, and planets in the universe that it is possible that life exists on one or more of them.

- But as far as we know right now, life exists only on Earth.

An artist's illustration depicts the first planet ever discovered in a triple-star system. The planet (upper left) is larger than Jupiter. The rocky surface of its moon (foreground) gleams in the light from the stars. The three stars (at right —the third star is setting) are 149 light-years from Earth.

How Will the Universe End?

Scientists do not know if the **universe** will ever end. Its fate may depend on the relationship between normal **matter, dark matter,** and **dark energy.** Dark matter causes visible matter to come together. Dark energy apparently makes the universe expand.

For about 9 billion years after the universe formed, the **gravity** of dark matter was stronger than the force of dark energy. As a result, the universe expanded at a slower rate. Then, for the next 5 billion years, the force of dark energy became stronger than the force of dark matter. The expansion of the universe began to speed up. **Astronomers** do not know why this happened.

Scientists think the universe may end in one of three ways. If the *density* of dark matter (amount of matter in a given space) remains the same, the universe will expand forever until galaxies are very far apart. If the density of dark energy increases, the expansion will speed up until all the galaxies are torn apart in a "big rip." But if the density of dark energy decreases, the universe will begin to shrink. All matter will come together in a single, tiny space. Scientists call this the "big crunch."

Three Possible Futures

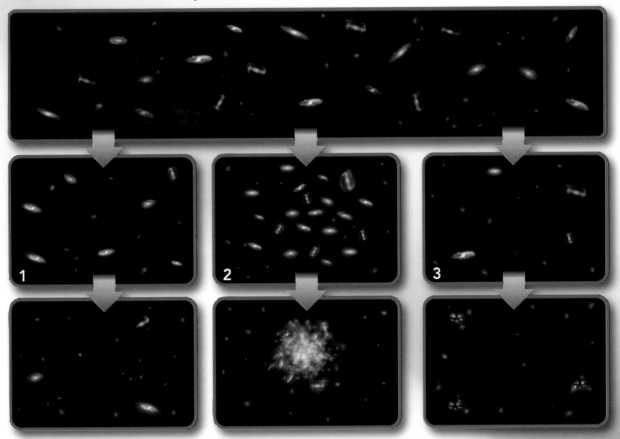

Highlights

- How the universe will end depends on the relationships among matter, dark matter, and dark energy.

- The universe may expand at a steady rate until all the galaxies are far apart; it may shrink until all matter is jammed together in a "big crunch"; or it may expand at greater and greater speeds until all matter flies apart in a "big rip."

Scientists think that the universe may change in one of three ways, depending on the nature of dark energy. If the density of dark energy remains the same (1), the universe will keep expanding until all the galaxies are very far apart. If the density of dark energy decreases (2), gravity will pull all the matter in the universe together into a "big crunch." And if the density of dark energy increases (3), the universe will expand at ever-greater speeds until all the galaxies are torn apart in a "big rip."

Glossary

asteroid A small body made of rock, carbon, or metal that orbits the sun. Most asteroids are between the orbits of Mars and Jupiter.

astronomer A scientist who studies stars and planets.

big bang The event that scientists think started the expansion of the universe about 13.7 billion years ago.

comet A small body made of dirt and ice that orbits the sun.

constellation A group of stars in a region of the sky.

dark energy A form of energy that apparently causes the universe to expand more and more rapidly.

dark matter The invisible substance that makes up most of the matter in the universe. Dark matter does not give off visible light, radio waves, X rays, or any other kind of electromagnetic energy. Astronomers know about dark matter only because of its effect on gravity.

electromagnetic energy Different forms of light with different levels of energy. The energy consists of particles called photons, which travel in waves.

elliptical Having the shape of an oval or flattened circle.

energy A quantity related to work, such as moving an object, or an object's giving off heat or light. Light, heat, and electricity are all forms of energy.

galaxy A group of billions of stars forming one system.

gas giant Any of four planets— Jupiter, Saturn, Uranus, and Neptune—made up mostly of gas and liquid.

gravity The effect of a force of attraction that acts between all objects because of their mass.

instrument Machines that scientifically measure and record such things as temperature or time.

light-year The distance that light travels in one year, equal to about 5.88 trillion miles (9.46 trillion kilometers). A jetliner traveling at a speed of 500 miles (800 kilometers) per hour would need to fly for 1.34 million years in order to travel one light-year.

mass The amount of matter a thing contains.

matter The substance, or material, of which all objects are made.

moon A smaller body that orbits a planet.

neutron star The smallest and densest type of star known. These stars give off powerful radio waves and X rays.

nuclear fusion reaction A process that produces energy in the sun's core, in which two atomic nuclei (centers) join to create a new, larger nucleus and give off energy in the process.

orbit The path that a smaller body takes around a larger body, such as the path that a planet takes around the sun. Also, to travel in an orbit.

planet A large, round body in space that orbits a star. A planet must have enough gravitational pull to clear other objects from the area of its orbit.

pulsar An object in space that gives off regular bursts of electromagnetic radiation. Pulsars received their name from these highly regular pulses. Scientists believe pulsars are a type of neutron star.

satellite An artificial satellite is an object built by people and launched into space, where it continuously orbits Earth or some other body.

solar system A group of bodies in space made up of a star and the planets and other objects orbiting around that star.

spectrum A band of visible light, or some other kind of radiation, arranged in order of wavelength. (Wavelength is the distance between successive wave crests.) A rainbow is a spectrum.

speed of light The rate at which light travels, which is 186,282 miles (299,792 kilometers) per second.

spiral A winding and gradually widening curve or coil.

star A huge, shining ball in space that produces a tremendous amount of visible light and other forms of energy.

supernova An exploding star (the plural is supernovae).

universe Everything that exists anywhere in space and time.

For More Information

Books

Beyond the Solar System by Steve Parker (Rosen Central, 2008)

Galaxies by Howard K. Trammel (Children's Press, 2010)

The Mysterious Universe: Supernovae, Dark Energy, and Black Holes by Ellen B. Jackson (Houghton Mifflin Books, 2008)

Universe by Robin Kerrod (Dorling Kindersley Publishing, 2009)

Web sites

Galaxies Galore, Games and More
http://amazing-space.stsci.edu/resources/explorations/galaxies-galore/

High Energy Groovie Movie
http://heasarc.gsfc.nasa.gov/docs/xte/outreach/HEG/groovie.html

How Black Holes Work
http://www.howstuffworks.com/black-hole.htm

NASA's The Universe
http://starchild.gsfc.nasa.gov/docs/StarChild/universe_level2/universe.html

Index